Believe in your Self

An ancient Sage in a modern world

A simple and practical guide to
bringing spirituality into daily life

by
Sharon Reef

D1118491

Believe in your Self

An ancient Sage in a modern world

A simple and practical guide to
bringing spirituality into daily life

by
Sharon Reef

INTERNATIONAL UNIVERSITY LINE
La Jolla, California

Library of Congress Cataloging-in-Publication Data

Reef, Sharon.
    Believe in your Self: An ancient Sage in a modern world / Sharon Reef
        p. ; cm.
        ISBN 0-9720774-1-3
        1. Taoist meditations--Juvenile literature. 2. Hygiene, Taoist--Juvenile
        literature. 3. Self-help techniques--Juvenile literature. I. Title.

    BL1942.8.R44 2003
    299.5'1444--dc22

                                2003026434
                                        CIP

© International University Line, 2004
Post Office Box 2525,
La Jolla, CA 92038-2525, USA

Library of Congress Catalog Card Number   2003026434

Printed in the United States of America

10 9 8 7 6 5 4 3 2 1

ISBN   0-9720774-1-3 $14.95   Softcover

Dedication

This book is dedicated with love and gratitude
to my Teacher, Wong Loh Sin See,
for showing me how to live

順天行道忠

慈忠信義禮倫節孝廉德堂

從地復禮義

Believe in your Self

Benevolence

Loyalty

Faith/Belief

Righteousness

Social Ritual

Proper Roles (Family and Society)

Female Principles

Filial Piety

Honesty

Enlightment

Altar

To follow the path on Earth, cultivate the self according to the laws of humanity and society.

To follow the path of Heaven, cultivate the Tao with diligence and sincerity of heart.

An ancient Sage in a modern world

Almighty God called a meeting of all the saints in heaven,
which included the leaders of all religions.
God despaired that the people of the world were lost,
having fallen away from the virtues of old.
He called upon Wong Loh Sin See of Confucianism
to carry out the task
of saving the people by teaching them the old virtues again.
Wong Loh Sin See fretted that the task was too great for him alone.
He was sure he would need assistance.
Tai Seong Loh Kwan (Lao-Tzu), who represents Taoism,
and Chai Teen Tai Sing (Chuang Tzu), who represents Buddhism,
immediately volunteered to assist Wong Loh Sin See.
Encouraged by the two saints, Wong Loh Sin See received the Decree
from God and came down to earth to carry out this mission—
the revival of the old virtues.

(As written in the Chee Chung Huay Temple, Singapore)

Believe in your Self

Acknowledgements

These people have taught me that human life is made up of relationships and I am humbly grateful to them all.

To my beloved children, Jessica and Alex. You fill my heart with love and my life with joy.

To Leong Tan for the gift of the Teacher, for the gift of love and the gift of a life together.

To Igor Tsigelny, without whose encouragement and belief these words would never have landed on paper; to Jennifer Medlin for true friendship and for the constant example of what it really means to be a good person; to Leanne Pate for her wisdom, laughter and gettin' real; to Suzanne Hooten and Gail Houk. You thought you were my students, but you were my teachers. To the entire Chee Chung Community for your patience, tolerance and acceptance.

To Kathleen Cunningham for being the best sister and friend I could ever want; to my mother Norma Burnett for love, comfort, support and, most importantly, for the gift of life; to Josephine Rutledge for helping me to navigate turbulent waters; to the Reif clan for a beautiful family life and to Jeffrey for true love and for setting me on a path to last a lifetime.

To Maharishi Mahesh Yogi for pointing the way to my Self.

Contents

Don't underestimate the significance of small things in your life
13

Love is to grow with.
Forgiveness is to let go with
14

Know where your off switch is.
Don't overextend yourself beyond
what is necessary
16

Know when enough is enough
18

It's hard to have an open heart
if we are heavy. If we can make ourselves
heavy we can also make ourselves light
20

It is in trying to be perfect
that we are imperfect
22

Heaven does not have a dead end road
for anyone
25

Enjoy your suffering
26

Believe in your Self

Contents   *xiii*

Connecting inside connects us outside
38

It is not how well you do something that matters. It's how open your heart is when you do it
40

To transcend in meditation is easy. To do it in life is difficult
41

Be simple and you will enjoy life
43

Cultivate the good in yourself
44

Be big of heart
46

Don't focus on the negative part of yourself. Focus on the strength
48

Don't think. Feel
50

The most important thing for humans is to believe in the Self. It is your foundation
51

All good things come from the heart
66

*Meditation is not what you can do, but what
you can accept*
67

*Peace comes when there is quiet.
Meditate every day*
70

Meditation comes from the heart
72

*Negative thoughts cause you to function from
negative energy and the body goes down*
73

*The senses used by the physical body can also
come from the heart. We can see, hear, touch,
feel and think from the hear*
75

*We have such a strong spiritual being inside us.
It is very important to spend time with it. If you
believe in it, it will believe in you*
78

*Patience, Tolerance and Acceptance are needed
in physical life as well as in spiritual life*
80

Believe in your Self

There is no wrong way to meditate.
Find yourself, find peace within yourself,
extend it to others
82

Strengthen the Self. Don't let the world outside
bring you down. Know that spiritual growth is
always taking place
83

What we have inside is a spiritual being and as
such deserves our respect and reverence
85

Don't ripple your own peace
86

Everyone has stress and difficulties. Pressure
can build and we need a tiny hole to let out
steam. Meditation is like that tiny hole
88

Doubt is like a shadow. It is better to strengthen
our beliefs than struggle with the doubts
91

Be Flexible. If we are extreme we will lock
ourselves in and not know how to get out
92

Contents

Awareness of being human is more important than awareness of the unknown
94

Maximum awareness comes from a place of stillness. To be aware does not mean having our antenna out all the time
96

Meditation does not give you answers, it gives you connection and connection gives you answers
98

Thought is energy
99

To know the presence of God, be present
101

When the awakening of your Self takes place, do not be afraid
103

Trust your Self, Trust your Heart
105

Compassion is the main ingredient of spiritual cultivation
107

Believe in your Self

Introduction

Every day is a beginning
Be a better person each day

A brief history lesson

In 1973 a discovery was made in China which was as important to Eastern culture as the Dead Sea Scrolls were to the West. A furnished tomb of a Han-Dynasty aristocrat was uncovered. This tomb, the Mawangdui, contained many riches, among which were ancient silk scrolls of Taoist texts. These texts were original manuscripts of the three schools of Taoism which thrived at the beginning of the Han Dynasty in 2nd Century BC. These philosophies were known as the Lao-Tzu, the Chuang-Tzu, and the Huang-Lao. Many texts of Lao-Tzu and Chuang-Tzu survived this period and are well known today. The Huang Lao teachings, however, had been lost for more than 2,000 years. This Huang Lao philosophy was extremely popular and influential in the courts of the Chinese rulers during the end of the warring states period and the beginning of the Han dynasty.

The rulers of this time believed that it was necessary for them to know how to align themselves with the forces of nature in order to be successful and ensure the survival of their people. The warring states period in China was one of great chaos and bloodshed, and the

Believe in your Self

individual spiritual development of the ruler was considered essential.

Eventually, with the rise of King Wen as ruler in the Han Dynasty, the Taoist teachings at court were replaced by Confucianism with its emphasis on social conduct as the form of government for China. The Taoist manuscripts of the court fell into disuse among the rulers and filtered down to the elite—such as the Mawangdui aristocrat whose tomb was recently discovered. This allowed the teachings to become more accessible to the people and, although the manuscripts stayed mostly with the elite, the teachings eventually made their way down to the common people. They became more religious in nature and were used as a means of spiritual cultivation.

It's a long way from China in 2nd century BC to the United States in the 1980s. Most of the teachings of Huang Lao Taoism were handed down through word of mouth from generation to generation from province to province. The people created temples in which to practice their religion and deified Chuang Tzu, Lao Tzu, and Huang Lao. Whether they were real persons or not is better left to scholarly debate, but the influence of Taoist teachings is widespread and takes many forms. These teachings of Huang Lao Taoism are as they came to me in the modern world of the United States.

Huang Lao today

The teachings of Huang Lao Taoism came to me through the channeling of this entity known as Wong Loh Sin See (Cantonese pronunciation). The temples of Wong Loh Sin See spread from southern China into Thailand and Malaysia along with the migration of the Chinese into these areas. The old ways of passing on the teachings through channeling is still practiced today, and in Asia is a very common and accepted form of teaching. The leader of each Temple has the trained ability to put himself into a trance, allowing the spirit of Wong Loh Sin See to take over his body in order to teach people of today. He serves the same purpose as our ministers or priests in the West. This channeling is viewed with fascination and skepticism in the West, but no matter, it's the teaching that counts, which is why those of us here in the States who follow this tradition simply call Wong Loh Sin See the Teacher. Sometimes we have to put our Western skepticism aside and judge for ourselves whether the message resonates as truth within us. Then we know that no matter the messenger, the message is helpful to us.

Believe in your Self

The message

The message of Wong Loh Sin See is quite simple and yet, at the same time, encompasses a vast body of knowledge. We are not taught to choose a spiritual life over a material life. We are not encouraged to renounce this world in favor of some future unknown possibility. We are taught to look at ourselves; to delve deep within our hearts and discover our own divine nature. This discovery is a journey. It doesn't happen all at once. Along the way we notice how we are operating in the world; the habits we've developed which cause pain to ourselves as well as hurt those we love. We come to realize that what we see with our eyes can be superficial, but that what we perceive with our hearts is real. We want to know what is real, therefore we develop the qualities of an open heart. We learn to meditate in order to feel who we really are and to become sensitive to our own energy. As we develop this subtle awareness of our energy we come into contact with our inner Self, that spirit, or soul, which resides within. We learn to just be, not controlling or forcing anything to happen. We are learning to really open ourselves up spiritually by diving deep into meditation, surrendering to our own energy and accepting what is there. We acknowledge its great, vast power for good. We come to surrender our ego to this higher inner Self and begin to trust it to guide us.

So this path is twofold. We learn to meditate and awaken our inner Self, and then to go back into life and endeavor to be a good person. We are given lots of encouragement and understanding of what it is to be a good person, of how important it is to our spiritual cultivation. The goal is to become able to integrate our spiritual life with the everyday mundane world in which we live. Everything in life is a lesson. Joy and sorrow can both be challenging. It takes courage to commit to a life of spiritual cultivation and growth, but isn't it, after all, why we are here?

Today, in America, Wong Loh Sin See is affectionately called Teacher. He is often asked about his origins and usually replies that it is not him we should be curious about, but ourselves. This is the purpose of all spiritual cultivation—to know and understand ourselves, to know that we have an inner Self which is here for a reason, to know that we are spirit, that we are here to grow that spirit and to become the best human being we can be.

The lofty principles which were studied by the ancient rulers of China remain the same for us: practice spiritual cultivation, learn to align the energies of the Self with the energies of Tao and flow with nature. This will allow for simplicity and naturalness in our actions. We will become able to open our heart, be unafraid, full of faith and trust, living simply and helping our fellow beings to do the same. The practice develops intuition and healing abilities because, through learning to surrender our ego to the divine energy of the universe and functioning from an open heart, we have access to our spiritual nature which is part of everything. Our feet must be anchored in the earth to be grounded and have a centered mind. Our heart must be anchored in heaven to know the spirit in things. When we do the work of humanity with a grounded, centered mind and an open spiritual heart, we are in the right place and life will be a blessing.

Believe in your Self

Prologue

I sit next to my husband on the floor of my new friend's living room. All furniture has been removed and I look around at 20 people sitting quietly on cushions facing the fireplace. We are looking at a small table with a teacup and a string of beads on it, next to a simple folded blanket. We wait for this Teacher we had heard so much about. Eventually a rather handsome Chinese man walks in and quietly sits down. He is introduced as Leong Tan and he channels the ancient sage Wong Loh Sin See. He says a few words of greeting, turns around and in a moment we feel a ripple of energy enter the room like the electricity in the air before a storm. He looks around the room, says a few words here and there. Then he looks at me and asks, "Why are you so sad?" I was married with 2 small children and the happiest I had ever been in my life. So why, when he said those words, did I feel all the sadness locked away in my heart come flooding up into my awareness? I had embarked on my journey of self discover with my Teacher.

The years brought many changes and challenges. My husband died of cancer a year after this first meeting with the Teacher—a pain from which I thought I would never recover. I did though eventually, and also eventually, I had the opportunity to travel with Leong and the Teacher across the country to workshops and retreats. I was very fortunate to have had 10 years of close personal training with Wong Loh Sin See. I will always be extremely grateful for this blessing. This book is not about me though. It is about the gems of wisdom spoken by Wong Loh Sin See. I am not a copious note taker. I prefer to allow what I need to learn just seep in as it will. I do, however, have a fondness for one-liners. Patience has never been my strong suit. My impatience needs to get to the point.

Whenever I heard the point in a succinct line or two, I jotted it down in a book I carried with me.

I would like to share the teachings of Wong Loh Sin See with you through these quotes—these "compressed files." The commentaries that follow are my attempts to decompress these files, to open my heart and see what wisdom has seeped in which I can share.

Sometimes we are forced to change,
sometimes we decide to change.
In any case change always comes.

Part I

EARTH

To follow the path on Earth
Cultivate the self according
To the laws of humanity
and society

Always come from the heart

This is the core of the teachings of Wong Loh Sin See. He refers to the inner Self as the heart. It is the center, the essence of our being. Our spiritual practice consists of going inward, finding our center, resting there, knowing what's there, accepting it, bringing it out into the world, and functioning from there. The inner Self is part of nature, part of the harmony and awesome power of nature. So when we connect with the Self we learn to flow naturally with it. To cultivate the Self is to allow it to grow naturally, to become more and more its highest nature. Our spiritual cultivation takes us to the perfection of our being where we become one with our spirit and all our actions spring naturally from that state of being.

Believe in your Self

Accept life as it is

How many of us can say, "yes, life is exactly the way I want it to be." Most of us have had periods of our life when we have felt this way, happy and content. We've also had the opposite when nothing seems to be going right; we're dissatisfied, frustrated, sad or lonely. Think back on your life. Even if you feel like you've had all one or the other, if you look honestly you'll find that you have had many periods of both good and bad times. Reflect back. Remember the main periods of your life. Can each era be characterized as a happy or unhappy time? Look within. During the happy times were there moments of sadness? Were there moments of happiness in the bad times? What you have lived so far is life. Accept it. What you're doing right now as you read this is life. Accept your life. It is *your* life. Just as the past has moved and changed, so will the future. Where you are at right now will change. So just be where you're at. Do what is required of your life today. Whatever your goals, plans, expectations or hopes for the future may be, it is not now. Now can be used to work toward the future if you wish, but don't pretend to be there now. Today is also not the past. So don't live there anymore either. Accept life as it is today, whether you are happy or unhappy with it. Acceptance does not mean you resign yourself to staying unhappy if that's where you are. It simply acknowledges reality. It doesn't mean we settle for less or stop hoping for better times. It means we look honestly at who we are, what is really happening in our life today, and how we have participated in the creation of it. We can do whatever we want to do to create a better life for ourselves, but without an honest assessment of where we are now, how effective will any action be? Accepting life as it is means living with the knowledge that the nature of life is change and we see ourselves for who we are.

In the center everything is equal so balance comes naturally.

Believe in your Self

Don't underestimate the significance of small things in your life

Everything that crosses our path is a chance for learning. In writing this book, I decided to just randomly open my notebook and write on the quote which was there. Today I opened to this one, but I didn't want to use it to start the book with. The one on the next page seemed so much more powerful. This one seemed so—small. When I realized my reluctance I had to laugh. Well, this is a lesson! I don't want to use the chosen quote because it's too simple, too small, too insignificant. It surely can't be one of the first ones. It seems that I'm being taught how to start this book properly—with simplicity and trust!

We are often waiting for the big moments of life—working toward goals, rushing forward and looking for something meaningful. Small things in life come and go so fast, so quietly, that they are often unnoticed. Doesn't our own life consist mainly of these small daily things? As we get older we often mourn the swiftness with which time passes. Would it go slower, be more meaningful, seem fuller if we paid attention? Let the small details of life be noticed by you today. Just for today really pay attention. Be present in your life. Tonight reflect on the day. Remember your experiences and count your blessings—no matter how small.

Love is to grow with.
Forgiveness is to let go with

Love and forgiveness—the most essential qualities of an open, spiritual heart. Why is it that we're all seeking love? Love is the highest expression of humanity, the most satisfying experience we can feel. There are many kinds of love; love between people requires many adjustments in each individual in order for the relationship itself to be the satisfying experience we desire. These adjustments in each individual will often force a person into growth. We grow in the qualities of compassion, acceptance and understanding. Through the development of these qualities we become a better human being, more fully capable of loving. So when Teacher says love is to grow with, perhaps he is saying that we give love and desire love in order to grow and to be better human beings. And as we grow into better human beings we are capable of greater love.

Forgiveness is to let go with. When we forgive, we let go of all the resentments we carry around with us. Our hearts cannot be light and free with this weight. We forgive ourselves for the mistakes we have made in the past, for the people we have hurt; we also forgive those who have made the mistake of hurting us. Forgiveness is not an easy thing; it requires letting go of the past and being willing to move on to new growth in the future. So remember the tools of love in your life. The next time you find yourself with the need to forgive, look to what you can

Believe in your Self

let go of to enable that forgiveness to take place. And the next time you find yourself in a new period of growth or knowing that you have the need to grow in a new direction look to find the love within you which will allow you to grow. Love and forgiveness are gifts that we can give to the people in our lives, but more importantly, they are the gifts we can give to ourselves to free us from the past and allow us grow into ourselves.

If you do not wish to destroy one another, you must forgive the one you consider to be your enemy.

Know where your off switch is.
Don't overextend yourself beyond what is necessary

Do you know where your off switch is? How often do you feel exhausted and need to shut down for awhile? What are your motives in giving your all and beyond? We want to do our best for people, for our work and for ourselves, but what is our best? Surely it is not overextending and depleting our own energy. Doing what we are called upon to do is all that is required of us. We don't have to do more to meet other people's expectations. This drive to do more comes from us, not the necessity of the job at hand.

Why then do we push ourselves? Do we feel somehow inadequate and need to prove something to ourselves or others? Are we so perfectionistic that it seems like nothing we do is ever good enough? Do we want to solve the problem, help the person, or complete the task all at once? Are the expectations we have of ourselves beyond the reality of our capabilities? Do we know our own limitations? Do we need to please people to feel liked? Thinking about and answering these questions will help us to see why we do what we do, even when it is not in our own best interest.

We exercise, eat well, sleep well, and meditate to

Believe in your Self

cultivate and increase our energy. How we use this energy is important and how long we use it is important. Learn to respect the limits of your own energy. Do what you can to build up and strengthen it and do what is right for you. You are responsible for yourself. You cannot be any good to anyone if you deplete yourself. One of my dear loved ones used to say at the end of a long day, "I've gone beyond myself." She knew when she had exceeded her limits and with this awareness could pull back, restore herself and perhaps next time turn the switch off earlier. We all overextend ourselves at times. It's part of being human. So get to know yourself by examining your nature, doing what is required of you to the best of your ability and nothing more. This is the natural flow of nature. To be nothing more or less than who you are.

Live life according to your beliefs.

Know when enough is enough

How many of us ask ourselves from time to time when is enough enough? It seems that no matter how much we do it's never enough and neither are we. Teacher often says "work is longer than life," meaning that there will always be more to do. It is up to us to know when to stop; when to take the time to recharge our batteries, to come back to ourselves, to go inside and connect with what is really important in our lives. No matter how pressing or how important our list of things to do is, nothing is more important than the spiritual cultivation of our inner Self. Truly, nothing is more important. If we are constantly looking for more, doing more, trying to be more, then we will never know the joy of satisfaction, of knowing when enough is enough. The more we cultivate what is inside of us, the more content we feel with who we are and the less that we feel we need in order to be satisfied.

This is of the utmost importance for those of us who are on a spiritual path and desiring to cultivate the inner Self. We must be able to say, 'this is enough; I am enough.'

Without this, the constant storm of desires prevents us from moving inward and being content with the inner, less tangible, spiritual world.

So when you feel the desires of the physical world pulling you outward into wanting more and more and feeling that you do not have enough, stop and look at what it is you desire. Is it something you need or is it

Believe in your Self

something that the world is pulling you out into wanting? The world is an endless chain of desires. Whatever we attain in this world does not compare to the satisfaction and joy of what we attain in our spiritual life. All happiness comes from within. All joy and satisfaction, all love comes from within. All the things that we truly desire are within us and attainable through going within. When we have inner satisfaction and joy, we are always content with whatever life has given us. All things come and go, but what we have inside will last forever and that's more than enough.

It is our own qualities which determine what we attract.

It's hard to have an open heart if we are heavy. If we can make ourselves heavy we can also make ourselves light

An open heart is always our spiritual goal. All the qualities we touch upon and cultivate in meditation rely on an open heart to make them real and to bring them out into the world. Wong Loh Sin See often gives us phrases like this one which provoke us into feeling something which lies buried inside—perhaps sad, misunderstood, angry or confused. Our response to this might be "I'm not making myself heavy. I have great sorrow and many worries making me heavy. If I could lighten up I would. I feel that I am doing everything I can. Why is he asking me to do more?" Actually, we are not being asked to do more, we are being asked to do it differently.

Teacher makes us think. Starting with "If we can make ourselves heavy," we hear the implication that we might be doing this to ourselves. Yes, there are those life circumstances which cause us pain and we need to have appropriate responses to them. We need to feel our genuine feelings. We should be aware, though, that we also have the potential to add to our suffering, by thinking too much, dwelling too long and getting stuck. We also have the potential to get beyond our pain, seek the help we need to get unstuck and change our thinking. Life can

Believe in your Self

bring us many sorrows and worries which, if "taken to heart," can cause us to feel heavy, as if a weight were pressing down on us. If we constantly feed these sorrows or worries with our thoughts, we will quickly become "overweight." Just as we can make our bodies heavy by eating too much of the wrong kinds of food, we can also make our spirit heavy with too much negative thinking. We can lighten up by eating better, eating less, thinking better and thinking less. Of course this is not easy to do when we have been caught up in bad habits. We will not change overnight. Change requires patience. But first it requires a decision—the decision to change. We are not wrong in thinking that if we could do it ourselves we would have by now. Help and guidance are needed and they are there for the asking. Reach out to your spiritual connection—to that which is greater than you are. Admit your humanity, seek your spirituality. Sincerely desire to become a better human being and the help you need will be there. You will learn to soften your burdens, allow your heart to open and to become light—as light as the spirit which you are.

It is in trying to be perfect that we are imperfect

How many of us have the belief that we have to be perfect, that we have to do everything right? We say things like: the perfect job, a perfect flower, a perfect specimen of a man, perfect example, perfection of the breed, etc. What does it mean to be perfect? Everywhere around us, especially in these days of worldwide media, we see examples of what we are told is perfection. The perfect diet, the ideal weight and body fat, perfect exercise, the right way to communicate, to "do" relationships, raise children, grow flowers, do our job, express love, express anger. What's the right attitude towards money, the environment, helping our fellow man? How do we best pursue our spiritual cultivation, find our passion, follow our hearts, don't worry and be happy? We're exhausted perfectionists, exhausted and often depressed. These feelings lead us to want to seek happiness. We know when we are in a bad place, often feeling sad and lonely. So off we go again, this time doing what we know is good for us. "Exercise more and I'll feel better, so work it into the schedule." "Family meals are important to raising healthy children, so fit it into the schedule." "Meditation is important for me, so make time for it." Now we begin adding all the things we know are good for us on top of trying harder at everything we don't feel "good enough" at. Something has to give and usually it's our health and/or our sanity.

Believe in your Self

Instead of losing ourselves, why not just give up being the perfect person trying to lead the perfect life? I'm back to the dictionary again. The definition of perfect is: lacking nothing essential to the whole, complete in its nature, being without defect, flawless, faultless. We, as human beings, are born to make mistakes through which we learn and grow. We are not finished products, but are works in progress. It is not our nature to be flawless. In making mistakes we are being naturally human—"complete in our nature." So if it's natural for a human being to make mistakes, then we must be perfect in this sense. We are not, however, flawless. Having flaws, we are not dictionary perfect. Good! We are thus perfect human beings, true to our nature, just as the rose, whether perfect or flawed, is simply true to its nature. So what do we do with all this? Take it easy! It is not necessary to strive so much. Trying to become perfect, or make our surroundings perfect, so that we can be happy, is against our human nature. "In trying to be perfect we become imperfect."

The next time you find yourself striving for perfection—STOP—ask yourself 'how important is this?' and 'what is it costing me in terms of my well-being?' Get off the treadmill of expectations and find simplicity in life. We've all heard that the simplest things in life are free. This does not only mean free from financial cost. The simplest things in life are also free from worry, stress and fear. Be true to your inner nature, flow easily with life, do the best you can with what you have and then let it go. We are not all that powerful. We have a deep spiritual life that guides us in what is important for us to do. That spiritual self is connected to God, to the universe, which certainly is "perfectly" capable of helping us. We don't have to try so hard. In spending time with ourselves in meditation, enjoying our own company, we experience the feeling of completeness and wholeness without doing a thing. For that is who we are. Our nature is perfectly at peace just being Human.

Be human. Live from the goodness and kindness of your heart.

Believe in your Self

Heaven does not have a dead end road for anyone

There may be times when we feel we have hit bottom. We feel we have lost more than we can bear, failed too many times, or a situation has gotten so bad we see no way out. We lose hope and want to give up. Life seems to have come to an end and we just can't go on. Indeed, at these times, life as we know it *has* come to an end. All our best efforts to go back to the way it was have no results. In fact, resisting where we are only digs us in a deeper hole. Life does not go back, it goes forward even when it seems like it's only going down. If you watch the cycles of nature you will see that winter always comes and things always have their end. Absolutely nothing alive lasts forever, but nature itself, which contains all this life, never ends. Spring comes and new life bursts forth, nurtured by that which has died. Ancient peoples lived within this cycle of nature and learned from it. In our modern world we are more distant from nature than they were, but it's always there if we look and notice. There is a cycle, constantly revolving, never ending, but only changing. In the container of our own lives tragedies happen, people die, relationships end, jobs and money are lost, but life does not end. Identify with the life within you that is ongoing. Cling to your inner Self. You always have you. You always have life.

Enjoy your suffering

This simple, annoying statement has many levels of meaning, just as we have many levels of awareness. With which level of awareness will you choose to look at life? Will it be from an angry, resentful, blaming attitude? Will you become sad, depressed, or hopeless? As humans we naturally experience all of these emotions. We know that suffering is a part of life. Our suffering pushes us along a progressive path through, and hopefully to the end of, them all until we reach the higher human qualities of acceptance, surrender forgiveness, love, understanding and compassion.

What do we usually do when our suffering becomes so great that it's almost intolerable; when we experience serious physical or mental illness, the death or loss of a loved one, loss of our wealth or security? Suddenly small things which seemed so important shrink to insignificance. We focus on what really matters to us in life. We look for meaning. We ask questions, look for answers. We seek help. We pray. Our lives become simplified. We become open to new ways of looking at life, at living life. People often adopt a complete change in lifestyle as a result of tragedy. Most importantly, we look within and ask, "who am I? Why am I here? How do I want to live my life?" We ask the questions we were born to ask and we set foot on the path to our inner world, the world of spirit, the world of God, the real world. Enjoy your journey.

Believe in your Self

Planning in life is okay. Sometimes though, our inside has a different agenda than our outside. Go with what your inside wants you to do

Life appears to need managing. We want to accomplish things, acquire things, and set goals which is all okay, but how much of it is a necessary part of living life? As a child most of us were trained to go to school and get good grades so that we could go to college and get more good grades so that we could go to work and get a good job, so that we could earn good incomes and have what we want in life. Most of us did that. We studied, we worked, we accomplished and acquired. Along the way we found love, we lost love and found it again. We had health, became ill and regained health again. Life seems to go its own way despite our planning. Situations over which we have no control present themselves to us. We learn and grow; we make new decisions, set new goals and make new plans. It's as if we are planning and directing our lives, and at the same time something else is going on. The cycle of life is going on and it sometimes causes us to stop, change course, and deal with situations we never dreamed would have happened to us. We change and life changes.

We often go through a lot of emotional upheaval when we find obstacles in our planned path. We don't want things to change. We don't want to go through pain. What happens to you when these obstacles are put in your path? Think back to times when your plans have been thwarted. How have you reacted? With frustration and anger? With a lot of thinking and looking for a solution? With fear and confusion? Do you run away from the situation through procrastination or escape to other activities? Do you get determined to see your way through and keep trying harder and harder to "make it work?" Whatever we do, we often find the problem doesn't go away. It keeps recurring until we learn the lesson we are meant to learn, until finally we change. We try to see reality for what it is and accept it. Accepting it doesn't mean we give up or approve of what's happening. It simply means we accept the reality of it. We know what we are dealing with; only then can appropriate change happen. We look more closely at ourselves, at our motives and reactions. We often find that our old, familiar ways of doing things just don't work anymore. There are old wounds and old pain calling for our attention. There is healing that needs to be done. So we begin with patience, acceptance, and asking for help. We learn from others, get more in touch with ourselves, notice how we feel and react, let go, and finally trust our intuition. We become open to new ways of doing things, which will come to us when we surrender and admit we don't know it all.

Our small self, our ego, does not have all the answers. Our spirit, that which is inside us and which is connected to the infinite intelligence of the universe, is not limited and all solutions will come from there. Planning

Believe in your Self

and setting goals gives us a structure and a framework for life to happen in. What happens in that frame comes from inside. Our spirit came into this world with an agenda, knowing what it wants to achieve in this life, where it wants to go and what lessons need to be learned. This agenda will take place no matter what we plan. Life becomes simple and easier if we are flexible, if we accept that what comes our way is uniquely tailored to suit our needs. These things come to us with love because some part of us has chosen to grow, has committed to becoming a better human being and to aligning with the higher Self within us. Don't always expect things to go as planned. When problems arise, know that they are part of the big plan. Meditate, get to know your inner Self and connect with it. Become a part of the cycle. Begin to function from your heart, naturally and spontaneously. Strengthen yourself. Learn acceptance, patience, tolerance, faith, and trust. Notice how things work out and you will probably find that you have grown in acquiring these virtues. You have become a better, stronger person because of the obstacles to your plan. Smile and, as Wong Loh Sin See would say, "be grateful for your suffering."

You are special and you are not special. Don't compare yourself to anyone else

Everyone wants to be special and they are—to themselves, to family and friends. We want also to be special to God and to our teacher. We have been given special gifts to use in life, hopefully for the good. Something in us knows that we are special—our inner Self is special. Without knowledge of and connection to this Self, we want to apply this "specialness" to our ego. To know our strengths and weaknesses gives us true knowledge of who we are and we can feel good about ourselves. There are always people better than us and worse than us. If we compare ourselves to those better than us, our self-esteem diminishes. Envy and greed creep in. Negative attributes that we don't want can become part of us. If we compare ourselves to those worse than us, our ego becomes inflated and we become vain, prideful and judgmental. We think we're special. In spiritual cultivation we strive to become simple, humble, virtuous, strong human beings. Comparing ourselves to others and feeling either less than or more than others develops negative qualities in us which will only cause us unnecessary pain and suffering. We will have more work to do on ourselves and more faults to overcome. Do we really need to add to what we already have? There is no need to compare. Be content with who you are. Make the effort to know yourself, appreciate yourself, use your gifts and be at peace. Being special really doesn't matter.

Believe in your Self

Of all the people you want to be nice to, be nice to you

It's the holiday season and I see people driving around and walking through shops with impatient scowls on their faces. They don't seem to be enjoying what they are doing. They're good people wanting to give gifts to friends and loved ones. Their hearts are in the right place but they also seem empty or starving or in great need of being given to themselves. So many of us have good hearts and are willing to give and to help others. Why is it then that this giving can sometimes lead to exhaustion and resentment, feeling unappreciated and sad? We often wonder 'what about me, what about my needs?' Well what about them? Who knows what you want and need better than you do? Are you as kind to yourself as you want others to be to you? Are you nice to yourself? Do you love who you are and appreciate what you do? Life can be easier and simpler if we value who we are more than what we do. When we value ourselves and take care of our needs we are more complete, feel happier and have more to give to those we love. It's a wonderful thing to want to be nice to people, just don't forget to start with being nice to yourself.

When all else fails—Patience!

How many countless times have I heard Teacher advise "Patience." Nothing makes me more impatient! I want things to improve right now. I want my discomfort over. I want to do, I want to act, I want to fix and resolve my problems. Time and time again I have bypassed patience in favor of action. I would try everything I could think of and when nothing worked, patiently waiting usually showed me that things work out in their own time. I've learned that I have to be willing to endure my discomfort while I stop automatically reacting, start to see what is happening, feel what I feel, meditate, pray, get centered, and wait for inner guidance. All these things cultivate patience. I've come to realize that everything is not up to me anyway. Imagine that! I don't have control over everything; I really only have control over me. I've learned to have faith and trust in that which is greater than me. God just might have a better plan than I could ever come up with if I will have the patience to allow it to unfold. My job is to be in harmony with that plan by being in harmony with myself. Today I still sometimes feel the insistent urge to react. Then I hear that word—Patience!

Believe in your Self

Smile as much as possible and keep life simple

This does not say to smile all the time or to smile when you don't mean it, but smile as much as possible. The emotions are fickle and can easily be swayed one way or the other. We don't need a reason to smile; instead, a smile can give us a reason to feel happy. When we smile the heart softens, and we feel good. This good feeling moves through us, through our smile and out into the world. It can touch another and softened and gladden their hearts also.

The smile is a simple thing and yet can do so much. It is effortless and can accomplish the same things that we so often put a lot of effort into achieving. It is an example of keeping life simple. We do not always have to do a lot or do things the hard way to feel good and to help others feel good. We all want happy lives. Look around you at all the ways people try to be happy. It seems like every activity, every advertisement, every book and every life choice has human happiness as its goal. Every day we are tempted with thousands of places to look for happiness. Why go through all that when everything we need is inside us. Right now there is something you can see or hear or feel that you can enjoy. Notice what that is and smile. Let the warmth in your heart lead you to its source. That smile is inside you and in the simple things of life. If we complicate our lives with too many things it becomes harder to find the joy. So be simple and smile as much as possible. You will be happier.

Let go of fear and the heart will open

Fear by its very nature wants to hang on. All letting go is impossible with fear holding the reins. To let go requires faith—faith in the infinite power of the universe and faith in the infinite power within us. Fear is a natural part of human nature. It protects us when used as nature intended. However, most of our fears are irrational and stop us from becoming who we are meant to be. Our faith helps us to look our fear in the eye, accept it for what it is, and then begin to slowly let it go. As we let go of fear our heart naturally relaxes and opens with room for more love, more forgiveness, and more joy. This gradual process creates in us "bigness of heart" and we feel tremendous compassion. Through this bigness of heart we become a blessing to others and can do our part in helping to relieve suffering in the world. Remember that fear closes you off from yourself and others. It closes your energy so that it is not available to live life to the fullest. Let go of fear, allow the heart to open and grow big enough to encompass all the love you can possibly contain.

Individuals are here to find a place of peace within, a peace that will resonate forever

Peace seems to come and go. When we have it, we try to hang onto it, only to find that the effort itself destroys our peace. We also destroy our own peace when we become worked up and distraught about something. It is in the acceptance of what is that we find and retain our peace. No matter what happens, the way to peace is through acceptance. Acceptance does not mean we approve of what is happening; it means we stop resisting reality and accept what has happened to us. Of course this takes time and we go through stages to get there, but there is where we want to be.

With acceptance we then come back to our center. We meditate and allow the stresses of life to be released, then let go until we settle into that deep inner state of peace. It is always there inside of us. It does not come and go. *We* come and go. Life pulls us out and we are responsible for bringing ourselves back. Through meditation we practice constantly coming back to our center. Eventually we are able to stay there longer and longer until that peace permeates our being, resonates outward into the world and we help others to find their peace. It will not be lost when we die for we take this peace with us and it will resonate forever.

Human life is a gift.
Since we are human,
we are a gift.
Cherish yourself

Most Eastern belief systems stress the concept of reincarnation. Our souls live on forever and only through being born into human life do we have the opportunity to cultivate our Self and evolve into a higher form of existence. Human life is a vast schoolroom with many lessons and many opportunities for growth.

There are many souls waiting for the chance to reincarnate into human form. This is why Wong Loh Sin See says human life is a gift. We have been given the opportunity which all souls crave. No matter how difficult life gets, even if you feel you just don't want to go on anymore, remember your soul. It has a reason for being here and it needs its allotted time to accomplish its purpose. If we become so despondent that we cut our life short with suicide, Teacher says we make an immediate U-turn. Always remember that nothing lasts forever. Good times, bad times—the cycles of life continue to revolve and bad times will eventually get better especially when we cherish life. Realize that human life is a gift and that we are that gift. We have worth, if for no other reason than that we exist.

We have a coveted place on this earth. Our soul has

a purpose and whether we realize it or not doesn't matter all that much. What matters is that we value ourselves, that we cherish this life, and that we trust the process of life itself. Love and cherish yourself as only you can do.

Be patient with your growth. Growth is inevitable. Every new day there is a deeper awakening within you.

Say something good and it will always have a positive effect.

Connecting inside connects us outside

We live in a world of many people and yet have times when we feel very lonely and disconnected from it and from other people. We can feel alone in the midst of a crowd, alone and distant from our spouse and loved ones. So we seek ways to feel better, to alleviate the loneliness, to feel connected again. We're all familiar with the ways in which we do this—more social events, more time with people, new activities, new clubs to join. Sometimes we find connection again and sometimes we don't. When we do, eventually the feeling of separateness comes again and we again start searching. Maybe what we are feeling separate from is ourselves. Our dissatisfaction is inside us. Our hurts, pains, joys and memories are all inside us. Sometimes we feel less lonely when we are alone than when we are with people. This is a sign that it's time to move inward, to connect with our inner Self and to become whole. The feeling of connection comes from inside. Meditate every day, connect to yourself, and become whole. Let your physical, outer being step back and let

Believe in your Self

your spiritual, inner being come forth and make itself known to you. As you spend time with it each day you will find a feeling of wholeness begin to surface. You will take your Self with you wherever you go. Your connection inside leads you to connection with a Higher Power and you realize that spiritual energy underlies everything in the universe and you feel connected to everything—inside and out.

The deeper we go inside, the higher we ascend.

It is not how well you do something that matters.
It's how open your heart is when you do it

We often focus on perfection in whatever we do. Not a bad thing in and of itself, but what are our priorities? Perfection at all costs? As the saying goes, "what does it profit a man to have gained the world and lost his soul?" Our aim is to grow our spirit, our heart. We want to develop the qualities of the heart: love, compassion, forgiveness, joy, acceptance, patience, harmony, and tranquility. As we develop these qualities we want to live from the heart, using these qualities in whatever we do. Then true perfection comes. Union with the divine is connected to the heart. Actions from the heart are divine actions and as "perfect" as nature. The purpose of our cultivation is to purify this heart, grow in these qualities and then open up. Open the heart, let the love and compassion flow out. Help other suffering people to find their hearts. When we act with this open heart, all our actions we be well done.

To transcend in meditation is easy. To do it in life is difficult

When we meditate we step away from the world, go to a quiet place, close our eyes and, with reverence and a sincere desire for connection, we begin to go within. As we continue to meditate, letting go and accepting, we experience the transcendence of our spirit. We experience movement from the gross physical world to the lighter more subtle world of spirit. The only effort we put into this is to take a timeout to sit and practice. The rest happens on its own. It is quite easy and effortless.

Life however, presents us with many challenges and gives us many opportunities to see where we fall short of the person we wish to be. We want to grow and transcend beyond the person we are with our pettiness, our faults and our difficulties. We want to transcend beyond this small person and grow into the larger spiritual person we desire to be. This is more difficult than meditation and requires much more conscious effort on our part. For instance, when someone hurts us we must not hold on to grudges. To do so causes illness in us. We must transcend by being big of heart, forgiving and letting go. To be big of heart and to forgive is essential to our spiritual growth. This frees us and allows us to transcend ourselves.

We're on a spiritual path because we want to transcend

to a higher level of existence after this life. We will be able to do this through bigness of heart. So be kind with yourself; be kind, gentle and understanding with others. To take the transcendence which you have achieved in your meditation into your daily life is not easy. The way to do it is through living from the big heart which has been opening within you.

When life becomes disturbing, let go of it.
Be with your true Self.

Believe in your Self

Be simple and you will enjoy life

What is it to be simple? This is a cornerstone of the teachings of Wong Loh Sin See. It is not just to simplify life—to do less, be content, set priorities—but to be simple. Being anything is an inside job. It requires going inside and seeing ourselves for who we are right here and now; to honestly allow our nature to be made known to us, the good, bad and the ugly. It's ok because we are human; we accept that we no longer have to be perfect. We do not deny our shortcomings. We look at ourselves without judgment because we want to see who we really are. This gradual process starts with willingness. We don't need to approve or disapprove, fix or pat ourselves on the back. All that can come later. First we need awareness. Knowing that we will not judge or criticize ourselves we can begin to notice what we do, what we feel, how we react. We can sit in meditation and surrender to ourselves and practice just being, letting go and accepting. Being simple is to accept life, accept ourselves, do what we can and let go of the rest. Take it easy and enjoy life.

Cultivate the good in yourself

Today terrorists flew planes into the Twin Towers of the World Trade Center in New York and the Pentagon. So many innocent people were killed. We are all wondering how humans who profess to be spiritual people can do this. We are all wondering why there is such suffering in the world. We are all looking at our lives and asking what is really important. Human nature seems to be such that suffering brings us back to these questions time and time again. When everything is wonderful we forget and we get caught up in the pleasures of having more and more. Our lives become complicated and we move farther away from the simplicity of our spiritual selves. It often takes a crisis of some kind to prompt us to turn away from the distractions of the world and back to what really matters.

But still we ask ourselves, how can spiritual people do this kind of thing? All religions teach us to cultivate the good in ourselves. Spiritual energy is neutral, whole, containing everything. It is neither good nor bad. On the other hand, all of physical life is a polarity of opposites: hot & cold, light and dark, up and down etc. Together they comprise the whole. This is the meaning of the Yin/Yang symbol. ☯ As we grow spiritually, our spiritual energy increases, our power increases, our intuition and ability to affect people increases. We encounter the dualities in ourselves—the positive and negative aspects

Believe in your Self

of ourselves. We have the free will to go with either one and usually we do both to different degrees. Just because we meditate, just because we have a spiritual belief does not mean we will be good people. How will we choose to use this energy, this power which is increasing inside us? There is a reason why the emphasis of all religions is on being a good person. It is irresponsible of us to delve into spiritual practices without simultaneously seeking the wisdom to be a good human being. The more we practice, the more we need to focus on developing the highest human values in ourselves—compassion, forgiveness, acceptance, love. These qualities will grow in us naturally when we stay simple and humble in our spiritual cultivation. As we feel the good in us we want to put our attention on it and develop it more and more. We know from passing through the stormy depths of ourselves that we have a lot of potential for anger, hatred, greed, envy, etc. As human beings we have everything inside. It is up to us to choose what we put our attention on and what qualities we develop as a result. So as you cultivate your spiritual energy, simultaneously cultivate the good which you discover in yourself. Try not to judge others. Put your attention on becoming the best human being you can be.

Be big of heart

Let go of that which closes your heart, which shrinks it. It may seem like you are protecting yourself to close yourself off from people, but you also close yourself off from your Self. To be big of heart is to allow the heart to open, to feel all there is to feel. There will be pain—sorrow, anger, fear. There will also be pleasure—joy, confidence, love. Allow these feelings to come into your awareness. Don't hide from them with an ever shrinking, hardening heart. Allow them to swell within your heart, expanding it. Give your feelings room to move. They will move in and out. The heart will then continue to expand and grow big enough to let others in. As we let others in, we feel their pains and joys also. Our compassion grows, our understanding grows and our heart grows. We then become able to feel the qualities of a big heart—forgiveness, compassion, love, laughter, surrender and letting go.

Believe in your Self

Death is inevitable.

Live life to its fullest.

Do everything you want to do

and make peace everywhere.

Don't focus on the negative part of yourself.
Focus on the strength

This does not mean to ignore the negative aspects of ourselves. We want to be able to see and acknowledge whatever is true about us in order to truly know who we are. But many of us spend too much time always looking at what needs to be fixed and not enough time looking at our positive attributes. When we are aware and noticing how we live each day, we will find many good qualities and many strengths. However, these good qualities that we discover do not cancel out the negative. We still want to work at bettering ourselves in those areas. We can do that by noticing where we are strong and building on that, using our strength as our foundation.

If we are always looking at our weaknesses we start to feel bad. Do what you can, be easier on yourself and apply your strengths to areas of weakness. You will feel stronger, healthier and better about yourself. Here's an interesting exercise. Sit down with yourself when you are in a neutral state, perhaps just as you awaken in the morning or after meditation. Make a list of your strengths and weaknesses starting with your strengths. It doesn't have to be an exhaustive list, just whatever comes easily to mind. Make the two lists of equal length. Now, look over your list and pick five or six items that stand out to you as being predominant. Make another list

Believe in your Self

of just these few predominating traits. Now simply look at the two columns of this smaller list. Do the words seem related in any way? Can one of your strengths be used to improve a weakness? Can one of the strengths actually be contributing to weakness? For example, perhaps the word creative is in your positive column and dishonest is in the negative. Think a bit. Doesn't it take creativity to lie well? Or perhaps you have a good sense of humor and a bad temper. Can you focus on the humor in situations which makes you angry rather than on the anger? How many of our strengths can be used to overcome our weaknesses? Play with this. Notice your strengths. See the connections within yourself. Realize your whole being and love the crazy mix of your own humanity. Sometimes your weaknesses are really your strengths coming at you from another direction.

Our weaknesses are really our strengths coming at us from another direction.

Don't think. Feel

Over and over again we hear this advice from the Teacher, and it often seems the hardest to do as well as the most necessary. The brain thinks, the heart feels. Both are necessary and good, but our western life is out of balance on the thinking side. We seem to value thinking above all else. In order to feel, we must touch our hearts, open our hearts and allow what is there to express itself. What a process, and how opposite to the way most of us were brought up! We were taught to think, analyze, don't trust feelings, and hang on to everything. Do we do all this growing, learning, attaining knowledge, only to let go of it all? What's the point? We are being taught that sensing and feeling is necessary to our spiritual cultivation. We want to sense and feel our internal energy and the energy around us. In meditation we let go of thoughts and feel inside, becoming intimately connected with our Self and the Divine energy above us. We cultivate our ability to sense and feel in order to sharpen our intuition so that we may help others as well as instinctively know what to do to help ourselves. When we are able to empty ourselves and let go of what we "know," we become free to act in new and more powerful ways. We learn to flow with life as it is, letting go of the past and making room for today. Strangely, emptiness leaves access to it all. Seeing what needs to be done we are able to do it.

Believe in your Self

The most important thing for humans is to believe in the Self. It is your foundation

What does it mean to believe in the Self? Maybe we can start with what it doesn't mean. It doesn't mean we are always right or that we won't make mistakes. Belief in the Self does not mean we are, or have to be, totally self sufficient in all areas of life. It doesn't mean life will be a breeze if only we believe in our self, believe that we "can do it." It does not mean that if we try harder we can force life to go our way. What then does it mean? Perhaps it means that we believe in our innate goodness, in our ability to meet life's challenges, in our connection to nature and a higher power. We believe we have a purpose and that all of life, all that happens to us in life, is part of that purpose. We trust ourselves to find a path we believe in and follow it, knowing that it will help us to fulfill that purpose. Without this belief we often flounder on the rocks tossed about by the waves of life. We are pulled in all directions looking for satisfaction outside our self. But with belief we are like seaweed, we become anchored and flexible. Wherever life takes us, we will always have a strong, centered Self. Waves may toss us back and forth and yet we remain rooted in our foundation. Belief in the Self is the foundation upon which we build a strong spiritual life.

See a thing with joy and it will become joyful

I'm sitting in the backyard and wanting to write. I'm distracted by the wind, the sun going in and out, warm and cold, the plant brushing my arm. I stare in front of me and think about this quote. I'm looking at a very overgrown shrub towering over the roof and am distracted by the work I see I need to do—trimming, watering and mulching. OK, never mind, I bring myself back. "See a thing with joy." I look back at the shrub. How do I look at it with joy? I see the branches reaching upward toward the sky. Suddenly a space opens up in my heart. The thoughts of work move away and I just look and feel. The red flowers bursting open, are they bursting with joy? Do the branches love to dance in the wind and do the flowers welcome the bees? Do they open themselves and give their nectar with joy and love? How far down do the roots go? Are they warm and solid, inviting the nutrients of the earth, are they aware of the flowers? Do they long to be a flower and experience the air or are they quite smugly content to be roots and sustain the flower? All thoughts settle down then and I feel I am becoming one with the plant. I see the joy in the life of the shrub and I find joy within me.

Believe in your Self

Every day is a beginning

Be a better person each day.

Once you know what is not good for you, don't do it!

We spend a lot of time learning what is good for us. We read self help books, go into therapy, research nutrition and exercise regimes. Always asking what should I do, what is the right thing to do? This is sometimes a difficult and often confusing task. As we learn more, we wear ourselves out adding more and more "good" things. Many of us have learned that simplifying our lives helps. What could be simpler that to stop doing the things which we know are not good for us? And what could be more difficult? Life teaches us many lessons and if we pay attention, we learn what hurts us—what foods cause the body discomfort or illness, what people we feel bad around, what thoughts and actions cause us pain. Strange that it seems so much easier to do something than to stop doing something. We are all pressed for time, so maybe consider shifting your focus to stop doing what hurts you rather than doing more to feel better.

Love your parents. They brought you into this world and gave you the opportunity to have life. Give thanks for that

Many of us have "issues" around our parents. We didn't have the perfect childhood where we felt nurtured, protected, loved, accepted and approved of. As children we were innocent, vulnerable and needy. We grew into adulthood, discovered problem areas within us, often got therapy and realized that what happened in childhood is often at the root of our unhappiness or difficulties. Some of us have suffered abuse or violence, others criticism or neglect. We see that our beliefs about ourselves were shaped during those early years and we realize that we are angry, sad, scared or lonely. For a time we blame our parents for our lot in life, for "screwing us up", for not being the ideal, loving parents we wanted and still want. We avoid them, rail against them, complain about them and eventually, perhaps, we come to the understanding that they did the best they could with what they had. Hopefully, we then come to a place of forgiveness and letting go. All these stages of growth and awareness are good.

Wong Loh Sin See would have us look at the simple fact that we are alive, we have life and this life was given to us by our parents. Whatever else they did or didn't do we have this precious gift of life from them. We walk this earth and breathe this air thanks to them. We were souls waiting for the opportunity to live here on earth and they granted us that wish, fulfilled that need in us. We had that need to be here or we wouldn't be here. Our soul had the need and the desire for human life and it took two other humans to get us here. It took a woman willing to loan us her body for 9 months and allow it to nurture us and bring us to birth. We don't have to like these people or approve of them or their actions or their life. We can have our issues and work through them and whatever else we need to do. But have love and gratitude for the two human souls who made your life possible. You honor their life and more importantly you honor yours. You honor your heart and allow your soul to be in harmony with its purpose. Your soul chose those people. Let your heart thank them and be at peace with its choice. Then be on your way with what you need to do, for they not only gave you life but set the stage for the lessons you wished to learn.

Believe in your Self

Life's interferences are constant. It's best to make light of things

How often is it that we can achieve our plan without interference? Can we drive to our destination without slow traffic, red lights and other drivers getting in our way? Can we cook a meal without the phone ringing, have a phone conversation without interruption? Think about it. Most of the things we set out to do will have a distraction of some kind. How can we be at peace if we get upset every time we are interrupted or something goes wrong, every time life throws a monkey wrench into our plans? We meditate to find our center and to connect with the source of life, with the peace we can find inside. When we come out of meditation we keep some of that peace and take it with us into our daily life. We want to live life as much as possible in a calm, centered state of being. Make maintaining this peace a priority in your life, and when these interferences come your way make light of them. Accept them and do not become upset. Life's interferences are constant so why expect things to always go your way and react negatively when they don't? Why not expect the interferences to be there? Then when they come just lightly say "oh yes, here it is." Blend into it, adjust to it and continue on your way. Be aware that peace and happiness is your goal. There are enough major life crises to cause us pain and suffering. Don't let the small ones disturb your peace.

Humility allows us to grow

Wong Loh Sin See often reminds us that "once you think you know it all, that's all you know." Life has a way of creating situations which baffle us and ask us to be humble. When we refuse by thinking we know everything, then growth comes to a halt. We dig ourselves into our identity to such an extent that we become rigid—unable to flow with the events of life in a creative, flexible way. We cling to our idea of how it should be and use all our effort to control life to fit our wishes. We refuse to change and growth requires change. A plant does not grow without changing every day.

What does humility mean? It is not the same as being humiliated or shamed. It simply means we recognize that we are not always right; we do not always know what to do. We are often powerless to change a situation in our life. At these times if we will admit the truth, that we do not have all the answers, then we have achieved humility. Humility allows us to ask for help. Help is always there, and with it we see what we couldn't see before. Perhaps we see something in us that we weren't aware of, or we see more clearly what action is appropriate. Answers will come and we grow into wiser, more trusting and loving human beings.

Believe in your Self

Be at peace in the present

and the future will take care of itself.

Create wholeness in yourself by doing one thing at a time

I used to pride myself on my efficiency, being able to do 3 things at once. I got so much done, but where did it get me? What happened to me? I became exhausted and my mind was divided. I started making mistakes because I was not present. To do one thing at a time and be with that action alone with complete attention requires us to bring all of our self into one place. All our mental attention, all our physical action and all our senses are focused on one point. We become one pointed, we become whole. We are not divided. If the purpose of spiritual cultivation is to become one with our Self and the universe, then how we conduct our daily life is half the task. It is equally as important for our growth as meditation and spiritual practices. It is a spiritual practice to be with our self, doing the task at hand fully and completely. What we accomplish or create is not as important as who we are and who we become when we are engaged in action. We want to become whole, completely at one with ourselves, and this can happen when we are focusing on one thing at a time.

Believe in your Self

Find peace through the heart,

not the mind.

The mind is trouble.

The heart is peace.

Peace is at the heart of everything.

Conflict is on the outside.

Peace is on the inside.

Part II

HEAVEN

*To follow the path of Heaven
cultivate the Tao with
diligence and sincerity
of heart.*

Spiritual Awakening depends on people's willingness to be with themselves

At some point in life most of us will begin to feel dissatisfied. We have been working to take care of our needs and fulfill our desires as well as establish a place for ourselves in the world. We become good at our professions, marry, have a family, and acquire material comforts. We are involved in many activities and have many friends. Why then is there that nagging feeling of disappointment, of wanting something more, but we're not quite sure what. Along comes midlife crisis. Somehow it's all not working for us anymore. We start to doubt and question. Often some actual crises such as death, divorce or financial loss sends us into depression or despair. Or we just wake up one day and feel that we hate our life. Everything feels upside down. Why should this be? Why does this happen? Perhaps our inner Self starts knocking on the door saying, "hey, remember me? Let's get on with it!" So we begin to wonder, "Who am I really? I want to be myself. I want to know myself. Where am I going?" It

Believe in your Self

often takes a crisis of some kind to start asking these questions, or to ask them in a deeper way than we ever have before.

The spirit inside us has been suppressed or ignored since the innocence of childhood was socialized out of us. It wants to wake up. We want to become who we really are. So we develop a sincere desire to be with ourselves and get to know our deepest, most real Self. We go inside through meditation and enjoy our own company. The ego will put up all kinds of resistance of course. It does not want to be disregarded and so finds all kinds of reasons not to meditate—"not enough time, too tired, too much to do, nothing happens, I pray, I go to church, I don't need it, the body hurts, the mind won't stop thinking." All this will come up to pull us back to the familiar old ways. We need a sincere desire to be with ourselves to get beyond all this and to awaken to our full potential as a human being as well as a spiritual being. It takes time to get to know yourself but it's the best spent time of your life. It's worth everything to find the time to meditate. Your soul wants to awaken and to do so it needs your attention. Don't give in to all the chatter of the opposing ego. Life puts forth all sorts of interesting things to capture our attention, but through meditation you'll find that the most fascinating thing of all is your own inner Self. Be willing to spend time with yourself. How else to know who you really are and what your true purpose is in life? Are you willing to discover your authentic self?

All good things come from the heart

Wong Loh Sin See refers to heart as the inner Self—our feeling, sensing, highest Self; not necessarily emotions or the physical heart. We all have a being inside of us—spirit, soul, inner self, higher self, big self. No matter what you call it, it is that part of us which sees without the eyes, hears without the ears, senses without touch or smell or taste. It is without physical form. It is what we came into this world with and what we leave with. It is the Self we want to cultivate so that when we leave this earth we will transcend to a higher level of existence, and while we are here we may become a better person in order to help others. When we learn to come from the heart we are aligned with the forces of nature and what ever we do will be good and right.

> *Allow the heart to open.*
> *Give with an open heart.*
> *Don't be critical and judgmental.*

Believe in your Self

Meditation is not what you can do, but what you can accept

We want to learn to meditate and look for technique—how to do it! We want to do it right. We want to do it quickly. We want to make it happen.

But meditation is not something we make happen. It's something we allow to happen. There are many techniques we can use. A good technique is to start with breath, being aware of our breath. Breath is life. We pay attention to life within us. We breathe and become aware. Aware of our physical body, where is it tense, relaxed, painful? We accept the body; adjust if necessary and then let it be. Breathe. The rhythm of breath takes us inside. We become aware of our thoughts. We're thinking and its ok, we go back to our breath. Thoughts come and go like clouds passing by. We notice them, but don't entertain them. Don't try to force them away or get lost in them. Whenever we find ourselves thinking, we again have the opportunity to come back to ourselves, to our breath. We breathe in and out, relaxing more and more. We feel. We become aware of emotions. Maybe we feel sad, angry, lost, frustrated, happy, or calm. Whatever it is, we allow feelings to surface, experience them and let them go also.

All these parts of us—physical, mental and emotional—come into our awareness on their own. We do not look for them; we do not try to control them. We have done our part by sitting down and closing our eyes and paying attention to what's happening inside. We are willing to allow that which is inside to make itself known to us. When we first learn to meditate these familiar parts of us will dominate our awareness. They are accustomed to grabbing our attention. Eventually though, allowing whatever is there to just be there, not minding, just always coming back to the breath, we find pockets of silence. We are on our way inward to the most fascinating and fulfilling of all human journeys—the cultivation of the Self.

In serenity times stands still

and there is no need to rush.

Believe in your Self

It's easy for a simple person to

become complicated.

It's much harder for a complicated

person to become simple.

Peace comes when there is quiet. Meditate every day

Peace—we are all seeking peace. What is it, what does it feel like? What do we expect ultimate peace to be? Stop for a moment here, close your eyes and see what peace means to you. What circumstances are you in and how do you feel in your idea or ideal of peace? Close your eyes now...

Did you imagine feeling peace at the end of achieving a goal? Did you feel peace in a tranquil setting? Were you quiet? Was the environment quiet? Remember the last time you felt peaceful, what was happening? Or was it the absence of things happening? How long did it last? Peace is the root of happiness and peace is always quiet, tranquil.

We can begin to allow peace into our lives by allowing quiet in. Seek to sit quietly in a tranquil setting. Go into a room and close the door, close your eyes. Create peace in your surroundings by occasionally shutting out noise. All the noise we invite in to escape feeling lonely does not give us peace. We need to be alone with ourselves—the quiet is there. The storms are also there and when we are quiet we will feel them, but storms don't last. They always give way to the peace that just sits, quietly, allowing all things to come and go. Become deeply and quietly acquainted with your unmoving, unchangeable peace. Meditate every day. Make peace a priority. Go to your quiet place, close your eyes, and

Believe in your Self

meditate. Feel yourself. Let the storms come. Be patient as they rage. Notice when they wane and let them go. Ah, there—the peace will be very big, will begin to swell and engulf you. Make time to be still, to be quiet. Just be there—in peace.

Always be present with your heart.

Meditation comes from the heart

Meditation is not something we can do with our heads, it doesn't happen there. We start from there with whatever meditation technique we have been taught. All techniques have the same purpose; to help us make the transition from outer awareness to inner awareness. Once we get inside to our heart, our center, then meditation begins.

The brain is very good at doing the work of understanding the world around us. It is a necessary tool for negotiating life. The inner world, though, does not make much use of the brain. In fact, it can get in the way because it wants to lead and control. It can cause us to distort and limit the potential of our spiritual growth. Coming from the heart does not mean the heart of emotional feeling, but rather the heart of our soul, the inner world of subtle awareness, intuition and sensing. So meditation is a state of awareness, not a state of doing or thinking. It is also a state of feeling, but the feelings are subtle and what we feel is energy—the energy of the heart.

Believe in your Self

Negative thoughts cause you to function from negative energy and the body goes down

The mind is a powerful tool and we should respect the power of our thoughts. They really can create our reality. Try this little exercise to experience the power of your thoughts. Close your eyes and imagine being tremendously afraid, filled with the most fear you can imagine feeling. Then notice your body. What does it feel like? Is it tense and closed off? Where in your body do you feel these sensations? Do you feel like doing something? What is it that you feel like doing? Now let go of that. Completely relax the body. Next, take a minute to imagine being angry, the most angry you can imagine. Once again, check in with your body. How does it feel? Where do you feel it? Now let go of that also. Finally, imagine being wildly happy, absolutely bursting with joy and pleasure. How does your body feel now? What do you feel like doing? Do you feel the difference in your body that the thoughts of your mind generated? Did you notice the actions you felt like taking? Perhaps withdrawing and hiding in fear, lashing out and hurting in anger, or reaching out and embracing in happiness? Whatever you felt is uniquely your feeling, your experience of the effect of thoughts on your body and on your actions. You just experienced the truth, that your thoughts have power. Your thoughts have the power to regulate your state of being. We have positive and negative energy within us and the thoughts which we think have the power to activate this energy. The mind is always active and would like to control things. In living from the heart we take control of the mind so that our actions come not from the mind, but from the heart. Pay attention to your mind and guide it into positive thinking by following your heart. Try to avoid letting negative thoughts take hold and you will experience a more positive energetic and healthier body.

Don't focus too much on your suffering or it will engulf you.

Believe in your Self

The senses used by the physical body can also come from the heart. We can see, hear, touch, feel and think from the heart

There is much to be grateful for in life. If we can see, hear, walk and talk, then we can consider ourselves fortunate. A person who has lost one of the physical senses will often grow in the ability to use the others. The paralyzed woman in the wheelchair has developed a strong upper body that takes her where she needs to go. The blind man's hearing and sense of touch and perception enable him to see. The deaf child hears with her eyes and communicates with her whole body. The common thread in all cases is not only better use of the other senses but a heightened sense of awareness. The lack of stimulus into a physical sense allows the mind to create other pathways. Awareness and intuition increase to help guide the person.

When we meditate we reduce the flow of information from our senses. We close the eyes and move inward toward the nonphysical realm of awareness—the world of the spirit, the world of the heart. As we regularly take time to withdraw from physical life and be with our inner self, we become more and more accustomed to this world of feeling and sensing from within. We become aware of our nature, of who we are. We grow in belief and trust of what we have inside us. We become familiar with an expanding awareness, sensitivity and intuition. We begin to see from the heart. We see more than a person's physical form. We see the true Self behind that form. We hear the truth behind the words, touch the essence of their energy, and feel the depth of their emotions. When we walk into the woods, or into a house, we sense the energy of the place. We continue to trust this way of being. We don't try to make it happen. We allow it to happen naturally, which it will with regular daily practice and attention. Eventually we learn to combine the functions of the body and mind with this inner Self. We begin to become integrated so that now we "think" with our hearts as well as our minds; we see, feel and touch with our hearts. There is fullness to our life. Our inner world feels boundless and ever expanding. This in turn enlivens our outer world so that we really enjoy what the body and mind can experience. We embrace life. We begin to feel a peace, which underlies all our senses, and to know a joy that has no limits.

Believe in your Self

Extend harmony regardless of

whether or not it is received.

The extension of harmony will

bring you happiness and peace

We have such a strong spiritual being inside us. It is very important to spend time with it. If you believe in it, it will believe in you.

I spend time with my Spirit each day in meditation and have for almost 30 years. I know it has grown stronger and wiser and I trust it to guide me. The problem is that I'm stubborn. I often don't want to follow this guidance because "I" want to do something else. When I opened my notebook to the quote for today, the page I opened was blank.

The automatic writing I did following my meditation said to do nothing, look for nothing. But later, when I got a blank page to write about, I didn't trust that! Or more accurately, I didn't want to do nothing. I wanted to write. It had been a month since I wrote and I wanted to get back on track. So I went ahead and turned to the quote on the previous page of my notebook. The quote above is the one that was there. "If you believe in it, it will believe in you". I tried to write about it. I crossed out 2 lines, stopped and started. It didn't flow. Am I believing in my own spirit when I say no, I want to do this, instead of the guidance you're giving me? So I decided to write honestly about what was happening and suddenly all this came

Believe in your Self

out. This is flowing. What another lesson. I have to believe in my own spirit telling me "not today!"

It is difficult to harmonize with others until you can harmonize with yourself

Patience, Tolerance and Acceptance are needed in physical life as well as in spiritual life

The Chinese word for endurance and patience is the same. In English the word patience implies waiting, while endurance implies maintaining while doing something difficult—'How much can you take?' When we want to develop a stronger healthier body we need to do more than we currently do, so we try to increase our level of activity: more aerobic activity, heavier weights, more repetitions etc. We endure this extra effort because we know eventually that we will see results. We will continue to become stronger and healthier along the way. Sometimes we notice progress and sometimes we seem to hit a plateau. But we have patience with ourselves, with our bodies and keep on. Some of the activities we may like doing and some we may not, but we do what we know will work.

Spiritual growth is the same. We want to become internally strong, connected, and healthy so we do what we know works. We have faith in our path and endure the difficult times, knowing we are getting there even when it doesn't feel like it. We have a lot of patience, with ourselves, our Teacher, our path, our life. All of it requires patience and we just keep going, enjoying the rewards

Believe in your Self

when they are apparent, gently believing in ourselves when they are not. We accept what comes our way. Our Teacher is like our personal trainer. We accept that he knows how to guide us in our "workout." We do the work with a lot of tolerance for the aches and pains this sometimes brings us. We accept our choices and smile occasionally with pleasure because we have chosen to move along the path to our goal—to ourselves.

*Connect to the part of you
which has no fear*

There is no wrong way to meditate.
Find yourself, find peace within yourself, extend it to others

Mediation is simply being with your Self. In sitting quietly, noticing our breath coming in and out, we gradually slow down, move inward and find our Self. Not all at once, but a piece at a time. From this place of quiet stillness we learn to be at peace with what we find to be ourselves. This peace does not come all at once either. Sometimes we come to a block or a discovery of an unpleasant feeling, thought or sensation. With an attitude of acceptance, we allow that to come more and more into our awareness. We allow it to be. We may cry, we may feel agitated. We may scream out or we may resist everything we feel. It's all OK. Just allow whatever is there to be there—no judgments, no analysis, no 'head.' Only the heart accepting the self, having compassion and trust in the Self. We go through the same cycles as nature: calm, storms which cleanse, and then calm again. With time and patience, we find more and more peace within. As we go into the world of our daily lives, we reach out to others. Our deep inner peace is felt by them and we pass along the gift of Self to others.

Believe in your Self

Strengthen the Self. Don't let the world outside bring you down. Know that spiritual growth is always taking place

It's when things in our life are difficult and going "wrong" that we begin to get worn out. We focus so much of our energy on fixing the problem, avoiding the feelings, on trying and trying to get it right that we begin to feel tired—"sick and tired" literally. We feel scared or angry and try hard to resolve things so that we can feel better. We begin to lose ourselves. We don't have time for meditation or quiet time for ourselves. We want to fix the problem first.

This is the time to ask "where are my priorities?" Who is in control of my time—really? We may not feel like we have any control at all at such times, but we do. We can stop. We can just say stop and close the door for a little while, sit down and be with ourselves. Take a time out! We know that what is happening is a lesson for us; we know spiritual growth is taking place. We can reassure ourselves that we will get through this. Our connection to ourself and to that which we hold above us will see us through.

Then put the problem aside. Have compassion and love for yourself, this beautiful person so willing to grow up. Sit comfortably, close your eyes and connect with your growing inner Self. This is what will make you strong. Continue to do what you know is good and strengthening for you. Stay connected inside. Feel that you have a spiritual nature that has a life outside of this problem. Be with it—with its unbounded nature. Breath, relax. Then come back and deal with the problem as best you can. Have faith. Tomorrow you will be stronger.

When yoiu meditate feel yourself, then free yourself

Believe in your Self

What we have inside is a spiritual being and as such deserves our respect and reverence

When we meditate we are connecting to our inner spiritual Self. It is a higher aspect of our self which has its own wisdom and knows our purpose in life. Just as we respect a person of high wisdom who does great things for humanity, so we respect the wise one inside us. Just as we feel reverence for a holy person or for the saints, teachers, gurus, Christ or Buddha of our spiritual beliefs, so we feel reverence for the holiness which dwells within us. Regardless of our human issues or how we feel about ourselves as a person, we need to know that our spirit, our inner Self, is connected to the creative power of the universe and deserves our respect.

Always be present with your heart.

Don't ripple your own peace

It's wonderful to have given ourselves a timeout, to have meditated, found some acceptance and peace inside and to feel that sense of calm, that everything will be alright. We have connected with the infinite and feel our true spiritual nature. We know we are so much more than just this body, these emotions and this person. Or perhaps we have just meditated and fallen asleep. What bliss to drift away and feel that deep restful state of being. So now we say to ourselves, I'm going to go out into my day and keep this peace, not let anything bother me. Then the next slice of life comes our way. The dog mistook the carpet for a bathroom, the spouse sends a word of criticism your way, the children are needy, you can't find your keys, the car won't start, the computer is not cooperating. Whatever it is doesn't matter; something will be there to challenge us, to demand our attention. We'll go into action or reaction and begin to feel this ripple. We have allowed our peace to be disturbed by life's events. To balance out this natural process of life we go back to meditate in the evening and connect deeply to ourselves once again. Over and over we practice, like dipping the cloth into the dye, and more and more we are able to remain calm under any circumstances.

In the meantime, it is helpful to examine what our part is in this ripple. Between the event and the reaction what happens within us? Can we catch the thought or the feeling we had as we felt that ripple. The events of

Believe in your Self

life really have no power to disturb us. We disturb ourselves. Start to notice your thoughts when you are disturbed. What are your expectations, your interpretations? What is the voice in your head telling you? Is it true? Pay attention to yourself and just be aware of your thoughts. There is no need to fix anything yet. Just see how you are. How often do you ripple your own peace? We always have the choice to think differently, to act differently and to change our attitude. Notice the next time you want to throw that stone in your own peaceful pond. Or, when you suddenly find that the waters are choppy, maybe you will bring yourself to stillness. Stop thrashing about. You are the center of your world. When you stop and become centered, slow down and just feel the movement of your breath, your peace will be restored. Then again go out and practice. It's a slow gradual life process which requires persistence, faith and enjoyment of your ever-growing serenity.

Everyone has stress and difficulties. Pressure can build and we need a tiny hole to let out steam. Meditation is like that tiny hole

Meditation has many benefits. Our main purpose is to cultivate our spirit so that it may transcend to another level of existence and so that we may be of help to others. As we continue with our spiritual cultivation we discover that we're calmer in our daily lives. We may find that we do not react so strongly or take our difficulties as seriously.

At other times the effort of handling our stress and difficulties causes internal pressure to build up. We have improved and maybe we're not as explosive or reactionary as we used to be, but we are still human and the feelings and reactions to life can build up inside. This is quite natural; we just need a pressure valve. Nature builds up atmospheric pressure and thunderstorms result to release this pressure, the same for volcanoes and earthquakes. The human being also has natural outlets if we allow ourselves to be natural.

Physical activity releases the tension of the body and if we exercise as part of our daily routine we will regularly have this natural outlet. Meditation is an outlet

Believe in your Self

for us also, sometimes an emotional one. As we settle down and surrender to ourselves, then often our stresses will come to the surface and seek an outlet. This is why sometimes in meditation we may feel like crying or screaming or growling or sleeping or laughing.

Any number of things may happen in meditation. Silence, peace and divine connection are the goal and they will come, but often these stress releases will occur first. Nothing is forced by us, neither release nor calm. What ever happens in meditation we trust the process and allow it to happen. We let go of the meaning which the mind attempts to attach to these experiences. They are just part of our journey inward. Let them go through that tiny hole and release the pressures of life. There are much greater things awaiting us inside.

Wherever you go, take your Self with you

Believe in your Self

Doubt is like a shadow. It is better to strengthen our beliefs than struggle with the doubts

This implies that we have beliefs. Without beliefs the inevitable doubts of life will pull us in every direction. We will be without anchor. Deep inside we know this and we long to have something in life we can believe in. If you have been searching and searching from one thing to another maybe it's time to stop. Belief starts with us. We believe in ourselves first. Sit with yourself each day in meditation. Become familiar with the being inside this body. Get to know the quiet, strong inner Self that is your constant companion. Allow it to grow and mature into a friend you can rely on and believe in. From this connection to ourselves we connect to something higher and extend that belief. Belief and trust in ourselves, and in something above us, gives the anxiety and fears of life a place to land. A space is created within us where we realize we don't have to do it all alone. We have guidance within us and above us. So when doubt comes creeping around with its foggy confusion—doubt the doubts. Once you have belief, don't let it go. Strengthen it each day. Connect with it each day and it will always see you through. It doesn't mean you believe you are always right or cannot change. It is not rigid. It means you love yourself and have confidence in your innate goodness and ability to grow.

Be Flexible.
If we are extreme we will lock ourselves in and not know how to get out

Flexibility is as important in meditation as it is in life. When we meditate we can experience all sorts of things. By remaining neutral to what is happening we allow our inner Self to do what it needs to do for our growth. Meditation is not static; it changes just as life changes. Every meditation is a new experience. Sometimes we have very good experiences that we want to hang on to. Sometimes we may feel like nothing is happening and our mind comes in and wants a past experience. It wants to recreate it. We can be so fascinated by "wow" experiences that we want more of that. Our desires conflict with what is happening naturally and the result is confusion. When we want more we become extreme and unbalanced. In meditation we are working with our energy. When we push our energy to extremes we can lose our connection to ourselves. The natural flow of energy becomes locked up. We are stuck on one way of being and it becomes very difficult to move out of it. We do not progress this way. We build up intensity and become unstable. Being flexible is going with the flow of energy, letting go of the desire to control and accepting what is. So when you meditate, let go of control. Trust that beau-

Believe in your Self

tiful Self inside you. Let it lead you to a deeper understanding of yourself than your mind could ever give you.

The same is true in all areas of life. Spiritual cultivation is not just about meditating. It's about becoming a good person and learning to live from the heart. We learn to integrate our spiritual life and our physical life. This requires trust and a willingness to follow our inner guidance. Meditation puts us in touch with our inner Self and our intuition. We come to believe in that part of us and to trust it. We don't want to control life with our mind. Controlling life from our mind is very limiting. We combine the two, blend them together thereby opening ourselves to experience new and better things. The spirit has unlimited potential for growth. Try not to stubbornly cling to any idea or way of life. Be open to new experiences. When life requires action, act with belief in yourself. When the action is finished and there is nothing to do, stop, come back to you, to your center, and rest. The more we trust ourselves, the greater our connection becomes. There is always a way out of any situation we may find ourselves in if we are flexible enough to be guided.

Look for how you can be soft rather than how you can be hard.

Awareness of being human is more important than awareness of the unknown

Through meditation we touch the unknown. We meditate, enter the world of spirit and become fascinated by our experiences. This fascination is normal and often motivates us to continue in our practice to "see what will happen next." Curiosity about these side trips is fun and interesting but we don't want to follow them and allow them to detour us from our path. This is not a trip to Disneyland. It's easy to let curiosity of the unknown become our goal rather than curiosity of who we really are. It's tempting to go off into these new experiences and want to know more and more about the unknown spirit world. Countless books have been written to attempt to satisfy this curiosity in us. But the immensity and beauty of the spirit world resides within us. All possibilities reside within us, within our own spirit. So enjoy your experiences, but don't try to hang on to them. If you hang onto them, then you stop growing. You just start going around and enjoying the rides without getting anywhere. When you find yourself going off and following some pleasant and fascinating experience in meditation, always gently come back to yourself.

We are human beings and our lives are fraught with difficulties and problems. Meditation can be a great escape from our daily life. It is meant to be so blissful and

Believe in your Self

pleasant that we will want to return again and again. This journey back to God is why we are here. But this journey is also about being human. What we want to do is take the wisdom, the peace, the knowledge we gain in meditation back into our human experience and integrate the spiritual and human aspects of ourselves. We want to grow into who we really are. Awareness of the unknown comes as a natural byproduct of that growth. We don't have to go out in search of it.

Once you think you know life, it changes

Maximum awareness comes from a place of stillness. To be aware does not mean having our antenna out all the time

Our physical senses are limited in what they can perceive. We can only see what we're looking at, feel what is touching our skin. Meditation cultivates maximum awareness through taking us to a place of stillness. No matter what our experiences in meditation, we're always cultivating stillness. Even when we don't feel quiet or when we experience a lot of activity, there is always stillness underlying everything because we are going to our center. The center is always a place of stillness, just like the eye of a hurricane. When we meditate we go inside to our center. We can experience all that goes on with us and yet, by staying connected to our center, we are always connected to the stillness within. One of the greatest benefits of meditation is this gift of stillness. It is always there for us. This is one of the reasons why daily practice is so valuable. That stillness is cultivated so that it can be with us at all times.

From this stillness of the heart our intuition develops naturally. We feel and sense the energy around us and instinctively know how to respond. This natural

Believe in your Self

process only requires our trust and belief in the Self. We don't have to try to feel and sense by always having our antenna out. The thing about being natural is that we hardly notice it's happening. We don't consciously pick our foot up, move the hip forward, shift the weight and put the foot down each time we take a step. Once we learn to walk it's a natural process and while we're learning, we trust. Intuitive awareness is the same. It comes as a result of our cultivation. There is no need to force it.

In serenity times stands still and there is no need to rush.

*Meditation does not give
you answers,
it gives you connection
and connection gives you
answers*

I have often heard people say that when they have a problem they meditate on it and get answers. It is true that when we have a problem it helps tremendously to quiet ourselves, shut out all distractions, and allow the subconscious answers to bubble to the surface. Deep meditation, however, goes beyond this. When we meditate with acceptance and surrender, we completely put aside the cares of this physical life. We only want to go deeply into ourselves and connect to the infinite, unbounded spiritual nature of life. We let go of all striving, all earthly needs and desires. We knock on the door to our soul and surrender to its wisdom, allowing it to guide us in our connection. This inner journey acquaints us with, and connects us to, our own higher Self and from there we connect with the infinite where all things are possible.

Believe in your Self

Thought is energy

As our energy builds through spiritual cultivation, our thoughts become increasingly important to watch. Wong Loh Sin See is always emphasizing the importance of being a good person. Thoughts have the power to create, especially when we learn to be one with ourselves and the powerful energy we have inside. When we meditate, however, we do not want to put our attention on our thoughts. We want to let them be, let them come and go as they will. We keep our attention on what is happening inside. We feel the breath and stay with the energy we feel. The inner Self is where wisdom lies. Answers can come from there. We don't have to stop and write thoughts that come to us in meditation. Meditation cultivates the intuitive spirit which will guide us in the direction we need to go when the time is right. Trust in it and it will always be there. Be grounded as much as possible and allow thoughts to be in harmony with your internal energy. The mind is constantly thinking and thoughts do have power; they are not static, but are a form of energy which is always moving. When our thoughts are in harmony with our spiritual Self, they have the power to do a lot of good in the world. Thoughts which follow our inner energy are right and powerful. We want our brain to follow our heart, not the other way around. Thoughts on their own can be mixed with the impurities of ego, desire etc. and so we do not want the powerful spiritual energy we have cultivated to be led by the brain.

Following these thoughts can cause negativity and confusion in our life. It's important to realize the power of our thoughts and the power of our energy and always use them to do good.

Be simple in your approach to life and you will find peace

To know the presence of God, be present

This is my fervent wish, to feel God's presence everywhere, in everything. I meditate, I pray and I try to be a good person, all so that I may grow in my awareness of God's presence. I remember one day watching Teacher fold a shawl. There we were, a roomful of people awaiting his next profound word and he is apparently ignoring everyone. All his attention is on folding; carefully, corner to corner, smoothing out the fabric with each fold. It seemed to take forever but as we watched, we were drawn into the feeling of complete, 100% attention on this folding; drawn into the calmness, the sureness, the unhurried state of being. At one point he looked up, saw us all watching closely and smiled. The look and the smile were no longer on the shawl at all. His hands stopped and we felt 100% of his attention on us. We felt his Presence. He was there, we were there, nothing else. Only that moment and then back to folding the shawl into a tidy little bundle, setting it aside, and it was over—then he said, "Please meditate." The moment of connection passed and the lesson was learned. We learned better than any words could have taught us. If I had been looking out the window (which I often did), I would not have felt that presence. I had to be present with all my attention in order to experience it. Anyone who has ever spent time with the Teacher knows this intimate form of teaching. It cannot be learned from any book. It can, however, be practiced in our daily lives. We can strive to be present to every moment of our life with 100% attention. Be centered within yourself, aware of where you are and what you are doing. It's not easy. The distractions of life and of the mind are constant, but try to practice this. Being present is worth everything, because it is there that we find the presence of God.

Spiritual awakening opens

the door of the heart

Believe in your Self

When the awakening of your Self takes place, do not be afraid

Regular daily practice of meditation will awaken the inner Self. The energy which lies within us transcends the physical. It existed before this body was born and will exist after it dies. Many, many words have been written attempting to describe this realm of the spirit. All acknowledge that it is only through one's own experience that the unknown can become known. Listening to and reading about another's experiences does not make it ours. The purpose of spiritual cultivation is for our own self knowledge, growth and union with the divine. On our journey we will encounter many experiences of our Self. This awakening Self has aspects which are totally unfamiliar to our usual state of being. At first we can be fascinated by the "differentness" of what we feel. We talk about our experiences and are amazed by them. To practice with sincerity requires that we do not get caught up in these experiences. We let them go. As we go on with our years of practice, we find it to be more and more personal. We don't talk so much about it anymore, we just do it. As the energy continues to awaken and move we can begin to have strange experiences that may frighten us. At this point it is good to once again have an experienced teacher to guide us and reassure us. This is where the development of a strong faith and belief in our Self and our path becomes important. It can be a crisis point for many people. Fear and doubt creep in, and without faith and guidance some will give up their practice. Here, in this teaching, we are being reassured not to be afraid. It is only our Self we are encountering. Do not let the mind come in and create more fear. Just as we did with the first fascinating experiences, we don't hang on to them. When meditation is over, we go about our daily life letting go of everything. Believe in yourself, have faith in your strength and the strength of your spiritual connection. Seek the guidance of a teacher, the support of your peers and persevere. Beyond this turbulence is another level of awakening and there will once again be peace inside.

Be as natural as possible in meditation. Don't look for things to happen.

Believe in your Self

Trust your Self,
Trust your Heart

As we grow spiritually, we learn to trust our inner wisdom. The more we trust it, the more it grows. The spiritual world of the soul is linked to everything. It is in accord with the laws of nature which work things out perfectly. When we connect to our heart, then our inner Self will spontaneously do and say that which is correct for us. It will guide us in all things. In surrendering the ego and the mind, and living from the heart, we become aligned with our highest purpose. The personality becomes infused with spirit and the goal of integration takes place. The heart is our source and our connection. It is more wise and beautiful than we can imagine. In order to go beyond what we know, we have to step off into the unknown and this takes trust. The first steps are the hardest and require the most trust for we have no experience to base it on. We go with our "gut ", our intuition, that this is what we are meant to do. In trusting that first impulse of intuition and going with it, we set in motion the art of functioning from an open heart. We experience the sense of rightness in coming from there. We now have experience and continuing to trust will become easier with more and more experience. This is a two-way reciprocal relationship between our inner soul and our outer self. The more our outer self is able to connect with and function from the heart, the more our inner Self will grow. As we continue in our daily practice of meditation, sincerely connecting to our center which is the heart, our intuition becomes stronger and more accurate. We become more and more able to stay in touch with our inner Self and will instinctively know what to do—if we trust our Self.

Listen to your inner Self.
Follow its guidance and
allow nature to do what it
has to do

Believe in your Self

Compassion is the main ingredient of spiritual cultivation

All the teachings of Wong Loh Sin See are aimed at opening the heart and functioning from there. As we meditate we are developing our tools of trust, belief, feeling, sensing, letting go and surrendering in order that we may go deeper into the Self. All this practice on interacting with the Self will bring us into contact with the deepest layers of the heart from which the compassionate qualities of the spirit emerge. It is not enough, however, just to meditate and sense these things. Our practice is also to cultivate the best qualities of the human heart in our daily lives and to practice compassion, forgiveness, harmony, love, and understanding. As these qualities grow in our heart we extend ourselves to offer them to others. We use the combined energies of our heart to help ease the suffering of humanity in whatever way we can, always remembering that we are part of humanity. We need to ease our own suffering also by treating ourselves with compassion and living in harmony with our inner nature. Compassion is a direct result of our meditation, of getting to know ourselves and admitting our own shortcomings as a human being. Learning to love and forgive ourselves, we learn to love and forgive others. The open heart feels the suffering in everyone and longs to reach out. We must satisfy that longing. It is the other half of our spiritual growth and allows our hearts to unite with the heart of heaven, earth and humanity.

Faith is a master key.
It takes this key to open
the door of enlightenment

Believe in your Self

Spiritual Cultivation is a beautiful gift to humanity. Cultivate everyday

Being human is a gift. It may not seem like it at times, but life, with all of its ups and downs, is an opportunity for us to grow deeper into our spiritual selves. What does cultivation mean? I love to look words up in the dictionary and here's what I found. To cultivate is to prepare and improve, to refine, to make friends with, to nurture the growth of. What does nurture mean? To give loving care and attention, to feed, to help grow and develop. Spiritual cultivation is to give loving attention to our inner selves, to make friends with our spirit, to allow it to grow and to become more and more refined. Through meditation we realize the reality of this spirit within us. As with anyone we want to cultivate a relationship with, we spend time with it, get to know it, allow it freedom to express itself. We do not try to control it, have expectations or demands. It is the highest aspect of ourselves, the part of us that goes on living after this body has died away. It is part of God. It is our real self. We came into this world with it and we leave with it. Human life is the one form where this spirit can transcend itself to a higher realm of existence, where we can realize who we really are. So we are born with this precious gift, the opportunity to know and cultivate our spiritual selves, to elevate our soul. Meditation is a natural process. Once we sit down to meditate, there is not a lot of effort involved. It takes place on its own. As our spirit grows in energy and power we are able to do many things. Our intuition becomes more and more accurate as we learn to trust. We develop the ability to heal people with our energy. We are able to extend our energy out and experience the energy of nature. We become more and more one with ourselves and with all that is. Yes, being human and being able to cultivate ourselves is truly a gift, and gratitude flows naturally from an open heart.

Believe in your Self

Believe in your Self and your strength increases all the time

We hear Teacher say over and over again—you must believe in your Self. This refers to a deep fundamental belief in the goodness and kindness of your heart. We go through many changes in life which cause us to doubt ourselves. The doubting and questioning of our outer self is an ongoing process of life. It is how we see our mistakes and how we see where we want to grow. Our relationships and the lessons of life are fertile ground for getting to know who we are and learning to know ourselves.

But to truly know ourselves we want to go inside through meditation and discover the inner Self, the eternal, ever-present part of us which is connected to everything else in the universe. It is this inner Self which has all the wisdom, joy and strength which we seek. It is that spark of the divine in us. Through connecting with it we realize that we truly are a part of everything and everyone. We are not separate individual beings. We are part of all Being.

We have these realizations through our own experience and, through that experience, we begin to really believe in the power and majesty of our Self. We begin to feel, 'I am a part of everything, but I am also a universe unto myself. I am the center of my universe and as such I must believe in that center.' We develop a tender, reverent love and trust for our Self. We see the changes in our daily life when we follow our heart and intuition. As we allow ourselves to flow with nature, trusting and believing in our Self to guide us, we see that our ability to enjoy life and handle our problems strengthens all the time.

It is through belief that our strength increases and it is through direct experience that we come to truly believe. It is a belief in the importance of your core existence; it is to see yourself with love and compassion, to see the good in yourself. Seeing yourself in this light you become stronger, better able to see your shortcomings and make positive changes in your life. This creates an upward spiral of growth and strength and allows us to continue on our journey with abundant vitality and energy. It all begins with belief in your Self.

Be human.

Live from the goodness and

kindness of your heart.

Believe in your Self